BEST OF

Germany

★ ★ ★ ★ ★

Deutschland

INHALT |
CONTENTS

DER NORDEN |
THE NORTH

* Niedersachsen, Bremen, Schleswig-Holstein, Hamburg, Mecklenburg-Vorpommern

* Lower Saxony, Bremen, Schleswig-Holstein, Hamburg, Mecklenburg-Western Pomerania

Deutschlands Norden – das heißt nicht nur Wattenmeer, Sanddünen und traumhafte Strände. Das Gebiet zwischen Emden in Nordfriesland und der Insel Usedom in Mecklenburg-Vorpommern, zwischen Sylt in Schleswig-Holstein und der niedersächsischen Hauptstadt Hannover hat viel mehr zu bieten. Auf Schritt und Tritt begegnet man den stolzen Zeugen einer jahrhundertealten Geschichte – mittelalterlichen Kirchen und Burgen, gründerzeitlichen Seebädern und der selbstbewussten Kultur der Hansestädte. Zeugnisse moderner Architektur prägen das Bild ebenso wie Fachwerkbauten und Backsteingebäude.

The north of Germany – that's not only the Wadden Sea, sand dunes, and fantastic beaches. The area between Emden in North Frisia and the Isle of Usedom in Mecklenburg-Western Pomerania, between Sylt in Schleswig-Holstein and Hanover, the capital of Lower Saxony, has a lot more to offer. One comes permanently across the proud testimonies to a centuries-old history – medieval churches and castles, 19th-century seaside resorts and the self-confident culture of the Hanseatic cities. Examples of modern architecture and contemporary transport planning form the picture as well as half-timbered houses and red brick buildings.

Nordseeidyll: Leuchtturm in den Dünen des Lister Ellenbogens auf Sylt.

North Sea idyll: lighthouse on the dunes of the Lister Ellenbogen/Sylt.

‹ Während der Kitesurf-Trophy steigen über dem Brandenburger Strand bei Westerland auf Sylt Lenkdrachen wie Möwen empor.

During the kitesurfing trophy, kites soar like gulls above Brandenburg Beach near Westerland on Sylt.

‹ Dem Sylt des 18. Jahrhunderts begegnet man im Altfriesischen Haus in Keitum. Typisch für die insulare Wohnkultur ist die üppige Holzvertäfelung.

We meet 18th-century Sylt in the Altfriesisches Haus in Keitum. Typical for the insular way of living is the intricate wall panelling.

‹ Bedrohtes Naturdenkmal: Die »Lange Anna« war einst durch eine Felsbrücke mit der Insel Helgoland verbunden.

Endangered natural memorial: the »Lange Anna« was once connected to the mainland of Helgoland by a natural bridge of rock.

« Flach und schlank: die Insel Sylt mit ihrem 40 Kilometer langen Strand.

Flat and slender: the isle of Sylt with its 40-kilometre-long beach.

≽ Künstlich aufgeschütteter Wohnhügel: die Warft auf der nordfriesischen Hallig Südfall.

Man-made hillock: the Warft on the North Frisian Hallig of Südfall.

⌃ Holländer-Windmühle in Nebel auf der nordfriesischen Insel Amrum.

Dutch windmill in Nebel on the North Frisian isle of Amrum.

Fast trockenen Hufes durch die Nordsee: Kutschfahrt von Fuhlehörn durch das Weltnaturerbe Wattenmeer. ›

Through the North Sea on almost dry hooves: Carriage ride from Fuhlehörn through the mud-flats of the Wadden Sea, a World Heritage site.

Von den Segelschiffen am Anlege- »
steg des Westhafens blickt man auf
das Ostufer von Flensburg mit der
Kirche St. Jürgen.

From the sailboats in the western
port the view goes to the east shore
of Flensburg with St. Juergen's
Church.

Badevergnügen an der Ostsee mit »
den typischen Strandkörben – hier in
Kiel-Schilksee.

Beach life on the shores of the Baltic
Sea with typical beach chairs – here
in Kiel-Schilksee.

Der Nordermarkt ist der älteste ›
Marktplatz Flensburgs. Er wurde um
1200 von dem dänischen König Knut
VI. angelegt.

The Nordermarkt ist the oldest market place in Flensburg. It was estab-
lished around 1200 by the Danish
King Cnut VI.

‹ Mit fast acht Kilometern Uferlänge lädt der malerisch gelegene Trammer See nicht nur zum Baden, sondern auch zum Wandern ein.

With its eight-kilometre-long shoreline the picturesque Trammer Lake is inviting for both bathers and hikers.

‹ In der topfebenen Landschaft bei Petersdorf auf der Insel Fehmarn sind Bäume und Radfahrer dem Meereswind ausgesetzt.

Flat as a pancake: In the countryside near Petersdorf on the isle of Fehmarn trees and cyclists brave the sea wind.

‹ Die Fehmarnsund-Brücke verkürzt seit 1963 die sogenannte Vogelfluglinie von Hamburg nach Kopenhagen.

Since 1963, the Fehmarnsund bridge has shortened the so-called »Vogelfluglinie« route from Hamburg to Copenhagen.

« Der Selenter See ist das zweitgrößte Gewässer Schleswig-Holsteins.

Lake Selent is the second biggest body of water in Schleswig-Holstein.

« Königin Marie von Hannover war die Namensgeberin der Marienhöhe auf der ostfriesischen Insel Norderney.

The Marienhöhe on the East Frisian isle of Norderney is named after Queen Marie of Hanover.

‹ Badekarren ermöglichten in prüden Zeiten den direkten Zugang ins Wasser.

In more prudish times, bathing carts enabled direct access to the sea.

« Die Nordsee ist ein Eldorado für Windsurfer.

The North Sea is an Eldorado for wind-surfers.

‹ Das Inselhotel König am Kurplatz von Norderney.

The Inselhotel König at the Kurplatz of Norderney.

Der Ratsdelft ist Teil des Emdener ›
Hafens und dient heute verschiede-
nen Museumsschiffen als Liegeplatz.

The Ratsdelft is part of the port of
Emden and serves today as a berth
for various museum ships.

Blick vom Radarturm Bremerhaven: ›
der Museumshafen des Deutschen
Schifffahrtsmuseums und die Colum-
busstraße.

View from the radar tower in Bremerhaven: Museum port of the German
Maritime Museum and Columbus-
straße.

In festlicher Abendbeleuchtung er- ›
hebt sich das in Formen der Spätgotik
und der Renaissance erbaute Rathaus
von Bremen vor der Liebfrauenkirche.

Brightly illuminated at night, the
Gothic-Renaissance town hall of Bremen stands in front of Liebfrauen
church.

Von den Hamburger Alsterarkaden »
sieht man auf das neugotische Rathaus.

View from the Hamburg Alster arcades
towards the neo-Gothic town hall.

Zwischen dem Hamburger Fischerei- »
hafen und den Schiffswerften mit ihren Kränen steht seit 2005 das Wohn-
und Geschäftshaus Dockland.

Since 2005, the Dockland building
with apartments and offices has
stood between the Hamburg fishing
port and the shipyards with their
cranes.

Hamburger Naherholung: Vor der Ku- »
lisse des Hotels Atlantic am Hamburger Jungfernstieg gleiten Segelschif-
fe über die Außenalster.

Hamburg's local recreation: Sailing
boats gliding over the Außenalster
with the Hotel Atlantic on the Jungfernstieg as a backdrop.

Elegant reckt das Chilehaus, 1922 bis ›
1927 im Stil des Backsteinexpressio-
nismus erbaut, seine bugartige Nase
in das Hamburger Kontorhausviertel.

The Chilehaus, built from 1922 to
1929 in the local Expressionist style,
juts its ship's-bow nose into Hamburg's warehouse quarter.

‹ Travemünde, heute ein Stadtteil von Lübeck, wurde 1187 gegründet und wird dem 1802 verliehenen Titel »Seebad« bis heute gerecht.

Travemünde, today a suburb of Lübeck, was founded in 1187 and has had the title »seaside spa« since 1802.

‹ Einst Amtssitz, heute Kulturzentrum: das Haus Mecklenburg in Ratzeburg, ab 1690 als Fachwerk-Backsteinbau errichtet.

Once a seat of administration, today a cultural centre: Haus Mecklenburg in Ratzeburg, erected from 1690 as a half-timbered brick building.

‹ Kutschfahrt durch die blühende Lüneburger Heide.

Horse and carriage through the blooming Lüneburger Heide.

« Das Mittlere Holstentor, Lübecks imposantes Stadttor von 1478, entging 1863 knapp dem Abriss.

The Mittlere Holstentor, Lübeck's impressive city gate from 1478, escaped demolition in 1863.

Den größten Marktplatz Nord- »
deutschlands in Wismar dominiert
die »Wasserkunst«, ein geschützter
Stadtbrunnen.

The biggest market place in north
Germany in Wismar is dominated by
the covered city fountain »Wasserkunst« (Aquatic Art).

Schloss Schwerin: Zur einstigen Re- »
sidenz der Herzöge von Mecklenburg
gehören ausgedehnte Gartenanla-
gen.

The extensive gardens were once
part of the residence of the dukes of
Mecklenburg in Schwerin.

Die gotische Zisterzienserkirche von ›
Bad Doberan beherbergt einen berühmten Altar aus dem 14. Jahrhundert.

The Gothic Cistercian church in Bad
Doberan houses a famous altar of the
14th century.

⟨ Das Rathaus am Alten Markt ist das Wahrzeichen der Hansestadt Stralsund und ein Musterbeispiel der norddeutschen Backsteingotik.

The town hall at the Alter Markt is the landmark of the Hanseatic city of Stralsund and an example for north German redbrick-Gothic.

∧ Zwischen dem »Teepott« von 1967 und »Schusters Strandbar« ragt Warnemündes Leuchtturm empor. Er bewacht seit 1898 die Einfahrt in den engen Seekanal von Rostocks Seebad.

Between the »Teepott« of 1967 and »Schusters Strandbar« towers Warnemünde's lighthouse. Since 1898 it has guarded the entrance into Rostock's narrow seawater canal.

» Die berühmten Kreidefelsen von Rügen sind heute Teil eines Nationalparks auf der Halbinsel Jasmund.

Today, the famous chalk cliffs of Rügen are part of a national park on the Jasmund peninsula.

‹ Die »Blaue Scheune« in Hiddensee, ein typisch norddeutsches Hallenhaus, wird heute als Kunstgalerie genutzt.

The »Blaue Scheune« in Hiddensee, a typical north German Hallenhaus, is used today as an art gallery.

» Aus der Blütezeit der deutschen Bäderkultur: die Seebrücke des Ostseebades Sellin auf der Insel Rügen.

From the heyday of German sea bathing: the pier of the Baltic Sea resort Sellin on Rügen.

‹ Architektur im Kreis: der »Circus« in Putbus, 1828 von Fürst Wilhelm Malte I. in Auftrag gegeben.

Architecture in the round: The »Circus« in Putbus, commissioned by Prince Wilhelm Malte I in 1828.

Die Ebbe setzt kleine Fischerboote ›
auf trockenen Grund.

Ebb tide puts small fishing boats on
dry ground.

Moderne Pfahlbauten für das mon- ›
däne Strandleben: die Seebrücke in
Ahlbeck, eines der drei »Kaiserbä-
der« auf der Insel Usedom.

Modern pier construction for a glam-
orous beach life: the pier in Ahlbeck,
one of the three »imperial resorts« on
the isle of Usedom.

Enteignet, umgenutzt, privatisiert: ›
Das Wasserschloss Mellenthin auf
Usedom.

Expropriated, converted, privatised:
The moated castle of Mellenthin on
Usedom.

Die elegante Bäderarchitektur von »
Zinnowitz auf Usedom wurde nach
der Wende glanzvoll renoviert.

The elegant seaside architecture of
Zinnowitz (Usedom) was restored after
reunification to its former beauty.

‹ Ein kleines Juwel der Backsteingotik: die Dorfkirche von Ludorf aus dem 14. Jahrhundert.

A gem of redbrick Gothic: the 14th-century village church in Ludorf.

« Die Stadt Waren eignet sich bestens für die Erkundung der Müritz, des größten Sees Norddeutschlands.

Waren is the ideal base for discovering the Müritz, the largest lake in northern Germany.

‹ Das mecklenburgische Herzogs-schloss in Güstrow ist ein stolzes Zeugnis norddeutscher Renaissancebaukunst.

The ducal Mecklenburg residence in Güstrow is a proud witness to north German Renaissance architecture.

« Die idyllisch gelegene Stadt Plau am See wird von der mittelalterlichen Marienkirche überragt.

The pleasantly situated town Plau am See is overlooked by St. Mary's church.

Das Schloss Celle, eine typische Vier- ›
flügelanlage der Weserrenaissance,
war die Residenz der welfischen Herzöge von Braunschweig-Lüneburg.

Celle Palace, a typical four-winged
building in the local Renaissance
style, was the residence of the dukes
of Braunschweig-Lüneburg.

Die Stadt Wolfsburg wird geprägt von ›
den Volkswagen-Werken: Hier ein
abendlicher Blick auf das Kunden-
center und die beiden Autotürme.

Wolfsburg is a city dominated by the
Volkswagen company. Here a view of
the customer centre and the two car
towers.

Nach langer Bauzeit wurde das »
schlossartige, malerisch am Masch-
see gelegene Rathaus von Hannover
1913 schließlich eingeweiht – von Kaiser Wilhelm II. persönlich.

After a long construction period, the
palace-like town hall of Hanover, pic-
turesquely situated on the Masch
Lake, was personally inaugurated by
Kaiser Wilhelm II in 1913.

Die Kaiserpfalz in Goslar, im hohen »
Mittelalter erbaut, wurde als Symbol
imperialer Macht von den deutschen
Kaisern restauriert.

The Kaiserpfalz in Goslar, built in the
late Middle Ages, was restored by the
19th-century emperors as a symbol
of German imperial power.

Der berühmte Braunschweiger Löwe, ›
der von Herzog Heinrich dem Löwen
als Herrschaftszeichen aufgestellt
wurde, ist heute das Wahrzeichen der
Stadt.

The famous Brunswick Lion, erected
by Duke Henry the Lion as a symbol
of his rule, dominates the old residence complex and became the
town's symbol.

Blick in den Nonnenchor des Zister- »
zienserinnenklosters Wienhausen. Im
14. Jahrhundert fertiggestellt, ist er
komplett ausgemalt.

A view of the nuns' choir in the Cistercian church of Wienhausen. It was
completed in the 14th century and
entirely decorated with paintings.

Der Marktplatz der alten Bischofs- ›
stadt Hildesheim mit mächtigen
Fachwerkhäusern und dem Rolandbrunnen, der einen Stadtknecht zeigt.

The market square of Hildesheim, an
old episcopal seat, with impressive
timber-framed houses and the so-
called Rolandbrunnen, a fountain
with a sculpture of a defender of the
town.

DER OSTEN | THE EAST

* Brandenburg, Berlin, Sachsen-Anhalt, Thüringen, Sachsen

* Brandenburg, Berlin, Saxony-Anhalt, Thuringia, Saxony

Die Wiedervereinigung Deutschlands hatte auch die Wiederentdeckung des Ostens zur Folge. Neben Berlin, das seinen Platz im Bewusstsein der Deutschen stets bewahrt hatte, konnte man nun auch wieder den Zentralort der deutschen Klassik, die Wirkungsstätten Johann Sebastian Bachs, Martin Luthers und der Bauhauskünstler sowie bedeutende Gärten und Parks besuchen. Städte wie Dresden, Halle und Leipzig verstärkten ihre Anziehungskraft durch aufsehenerregende Wiederaufbaumaßnahmen. Das Elbsandsteingebirge, die Lausitz und das Erzgebirge wurden wieder zu attraktiven Reisezielen. Und immer noch gibt es hier viel Neues zu entdecken.

The reunification of Germany resulted in the re-discovery of East Germany. In addition to Berlin, which had always maintained its position in the awareness of the Germans, the centre of the German classical era, the domains of Johann Sebastian Bach, Martin Luther and the Bauhaus artists, as well as impressive gardens and parks, could now be re-visited. Cities like Dresden, Halle and Leipzig reinforced their attractiveness by means of sensational restoration campaigns and cultural heritage preservation. The Elbsandsteingebirge, the Lausitz, and the Erzgebirge again became tourist attractions. And there are still many other things to discover.

Blick vom Ferdinandstein im Elbsandsteingebirge auf die Basteibrücke.

View from the Ferdinandstein (Elbsandsteingebirge) to the Basteibrücke.

‹ Gegen Tuberkulose und Mietskasernennot: Die Hackeschen Höfe wurden 1907 eingeweiht. Mit ihren großen Fenstern und den Innenhöfen standen sie ganz im Zeichen der Lebensreform.

Against tuberculosis and miserable tenement housing: The Hackesche Höfe were officially opened in 1907. With their large windows and courts, they were dedicated to life reform.

‹ Das Zentrum Ostberlins: der »Alex« (Alexanderplatz) mit der 1969 eingeweihten Urania-Weltzeituhr.

The centre of Eastern Berlin: the »Alex« (Alexander Square) with the Urania world clock, erected in 1969.

‹ »Ohne Sorge«: Sein Potsdamer Sommerschloss nannte der eigenbrötlerische König Friedrich II. »Sanssouci«.

»Without cares«: The reclusive Prussian king Frederick II (the Great) called his summer palace in Potsdam »Sanssouci«.

« Die Kuppel des englischen Architekten Norman Foster bekrönt den alten, nach der Wiedervereinigung restaurierten Berliner Reichstag.

A dome by the English architect Norman Foster crowns the old Berlin Reichstag which was restored after reunification.

« Beim typischen »Umgebindehaus«
der Oberlausitz befreit ein Fachwerk-
gerüst die ebenerdige Blockstube
von der Last des Daches.

For the typical »Umgebindehaus« in
the Oberlausitz a half-timbered
framework relieves the ground level
blockhouse of the weight of its roof.

‹ Die Fluss- und Kanallandschaft des
Spreewalds – berühmt auch für seine
Gurken – lädt zu Paddeltouren ein.

The river and canal countryside of the
Spreewald – famous for its gherkins
– is perfect for a canoe trip.

« Nach englischem Muster: der Land-
schaftspark des Fürsten von Pückler-
Muskau in Bad Muskau, angelegt ab
1815.

Very British: the park landscape laid
out from 1815 by the Prince of Pück-
ler-Muskau in Bad Muskau.

‹ Die Kunst des Ostereis: Die westsla-
wische Minderheit der Sorben prägt
mit ihrem Brauchtum die Lausitz.

Artistic Easter eggs: the ancient customs of the Sorbs, a West Slavian
minority, are characteristic for the
Lausitz.

« Quedlinburgs Mittelalterarchitektur gehört seit 1992 zum Weltkulturerbe. Hier geht der Blick auf die Kirche St. Benedikti mit ihrem Westwerk.

Since 1992, Quedlinburg's medieval architecture has been World Heritage. A view of the church St Benedict with its westwork entrance.

‹ Über die Elbe hinweg geht der Blick auf den Magdeburger Dom, die imposante Grabkirche Kaiser Otto I.

View across the Elbe towards Magdeburg Cathedral, the impressive burial church of Emperor Otto I.

« Der Brocken ist der höchste Berg der Nordhälfte Deutschlands. Goethe hat ihn 1777 bestiegen. Heute lockt er im Winter die Skifahrer an.

The Brocken is the highest mountain in the northern part of Germany. Goethe climbed it in 1777. Today it attracts many skiers in winter.

‹ Malerisches Fachwerk prägt die Straßen der im anhaltinischen Teil des Harzes gelegenen Stadt Wernigerode.

Picturesque half-timbered buildings are typical for the appearance of Wernigerode, a town in the Anhalt part of the Harz.

Das Bauhaus, 1919 in Weimar ge- ›
gründet, wurde zum Laboratorium für
eine neue Ästhetik. Nach dem Umzug
entstand in Dessau 1926 das Bau-
hausgebäude.

The Bauhaus, founded in Weimar in
1919, became a laboratory for a new
aesthetical style. After the move to
Dessau in 1926, the Bauhaus building
was erected there.

Das Dessau-Wörlitzer Gartenreich »
wurde im fürstlichen Auftrag in der
zweiten Hälfte des 18. Jahrhunderts
angelegt. Seine scheinbare Natür-
lichkeit stand in gewolltem Kontrast
zu den starren Barockgärten der Zeit.

The gardens of Dessau-Wörlitz were
laid out at the request of a prince in
the second half of the 18th century.
Its apparent naturalness was in de-
sired contrast to the formality of Baroque gardens of the time.

^ Das Lutherhaus in Wittenberg ist das ehemalige Augustinerkloster, in dem der zukünftige Reformator Martin Luther seine Ausbildung erhielt und später als Privatmann wohnte.

The house of Luther in Wittenberg is the former Augustine Monastery, in which the reformer Martin Luther received his education and later privately resided.

Auf der Wartburg bei Eisenach, dem ⌐ Schauplatz des Sängerkriegs, lebte Martin Luther als »Junker Jörg«.

On the Wartburg near Eisenach, the arena of the »minstrels' contest«, Martin Luther lived under the alias of »Junker Jörg«.

Auf dem großen Marktplatz von Wittenberg steht das erste deutsche Denkmal für einen Nichtadligen – zu Ehren des Reformators Martin Luther.

On the big marketplace in Wittenberg the first monument to a German commoner stands in honour of the reformer Martin Luther.

Von ihrem Denkmal vor dem Natio- »
naltheater in Weimar aus blicken
Schiller und Goethe seit 1857 auf das
»deutsche Athen«.

From their monument in front of the
National Theatre in Weimar, Schiller
and Goethe look down on the »Ath-
ens of Germany«.

Als Goethe nach Weimar übersiedel- »
te, bezog er zunächst ein ehemaliges
Winzerhaus im Park an der Ilm, das
heute besichtigt werden kann.

When Goethe moved to Weimar, he
first occupied an earlier wine-grower's house in the park on the river Ilm
which can be visited today.

Architektonische Seltenheit: Die 1325 ›
errichtete und 1472 erneuerte Krä-
merbrücke in Erfurt gilt als längste
mit Häusern bebaute Brücke.

An architectural rarity: the Krämer
Bridge in Erfurt, first built in 1325 and
restored in 1472, is regarded as the
longest bridge with houses built on it.

Die Moritzburg in Halle ist eine beein- ›
druckende Burganlage. Die einstige
Residenz der Magdeburger Erzbischöfe dient heute als Museum.

The Moritzburg in Halle is an impressive fortress complex. Today, the former residence of the archbishops of
Magdeburg is a museum.

Vor dem neuen Leipziger Gewand- ›
haus, der Spielstätte des berühmten
Orchesters, erhebt sich der neobaro-
cke Mendebrunnen.

In front of the new Leipziger Gewand-
haus, home of the famous orchestra,
stands a neo-Baroque fountain, the
Mendebrunnen.

Steil ragen die eleganten Türme des ›
Ostchors des Naumburger Doms in
den Nachthimmel.

The elegant towers of Naumburg Cathedral's chancel rise steeply in the
evening sky.

In der Leipziger Nikolaikirche wirkten »
Luther und Bach. Hier fanden seit
1982 die zur Friedlichen Revolution
führenden Montagsgebete statt.

The Leipzig Nikolai Church was a do-
main of Luther and Bach. Here, from
1982, the Monday prayer meetings
took place which led to the Peaceful
Revolution.

‹ Blick über die Augustusbrücke auf die Altstadt von Dresden: in der Bildmitte die Kuppel der wiederhergestellten Frauenkirche.

View of the Augustus Bridge and the old quarter of Dresden: in the centre is the dome of the restored Frauenkirche.

‹ Die prachtvoll dekorierte Semperoper mit ihren vier Rängen ist das Haus der Sächsischen Staatsoper Dresden.

The richly decorated Semper Opera with its four tiers is the home of the famous Saxon State Opera Dresden.

‹ Der Kernbau von Schloss Pillnitz an der Elbe, ein Palais des machtbewussten Kurfürsten August des Starken.

The core building of Pillnitz Palace, a retreat of the powerful Elector August the Strong.

« Der Dresdner Neumarkt mit der Frauenkirche, die nach ihrer Zerstörung im Zweiten Weltkrieg zwischen 1996 und 2005 wieder aufgebaut wurde.

The Dresden Neumarkt (new market) with the Frauenkirche, which was reconstructed between 1996 and 2005 after its destruction in World War II.

Alljährlich zieht der Weihnachtsmarkt ›
auf dem Rathausplatz von Annaberg
im Erzgebirge zahlreiche Besucher
an.

Every year, the Christmas market on
the Rathausplatz in Annaberg in the
Erzgebirge attracts many visitors.

Blick über die Elbe auf den Burgberg »
der Porzellanstadt Meißen mit dem
Dom und der Albrechtsburg, der ers-
ten deutschen Schlossanlage.

View across the Elbe to the castle hill
in the porcelain town Meißen with its
cathedral and the first German palace complex.

Weltbekannt sind Holzfiguren aus ›
dem Erzgebirge: Räuchermännchen
und Nussknacker im Spielzeugdorf
Seiffen.

Wooden figures from the Erzgebirge
are world-famous: Räuchermännchen (incense burners) and nut
crackers in the toy village Seiffen.

Blick von der Festung Königstein, »
eine der größten Burgen Europas, auf
den Lilienstein.

View from the fortress Königstein,
one of the largest castles in Europe,
to the Lilienstein.

DER WESTEN | THE WEST

* Nordrhein-Westfalen, Hessen, Rheinland-Pfalz, Saarland

* North Rhine-Westphalia, Hesse, Rhineland-Palatinate, Saarland

Im Westen nichts Neues? Und ob: Zwischen Rheinland und Weserbergland begegnen dem Reisenden nicht nur seltene karolingische Steinbauten, barocke westfälische Wasserschlösser und bedeutende mittelalterliche Dome, sondern auch frühe Industriedenkmäler und aufregende zeitgenössische Architekturen. Museen, Konzerthäuser und Theater prägen das vielfältige kulturelle Leben der Städte und zeugen von mäzenatischem Wirken und philanthropischem Bürgersinn. Dass »der Westen« nicht einfach gleichbedeutend ist mit Ruhrgebiet und Wirtschaftsstandort belegen die bunten Stadtbilder ebenso wie die idyllischen Landschaften.

Nothing new in the west? You bet: Between the Rhineland and the Weser hill country visitors will not only come across Carolingian stone buildings, Baroque moated castles in Westphalia and renowned medieval cathedrals, they also see early industrial monuments and exciting contemporary architecture. Museums, concert halls, and theatres are striking examples of the versatile cultural life in the towns, and a testimony to private sponsorship and a philanthropical public spirit. Colourful town-life and an idyllic countryside show that the west of Germany is not simply synonymous with the Ruhr area and economic centres.

Die schönste Aussicht auf die Saar bietet sich vom Aussichtspunkt Cloef in Mettlach.

The most beautiful view of the Saar provides the viewpoint Cloef at Mettlach.

Der Medienhafen in Düsseldorf mit »
dem grazilen Fernsehturm und dem
neuen Zollhof, einem Bürogebäude
des amerikanischen Architekten
Frank Gehry.

The Medienhafen in Düsseldorf with
the slender TV tower and the new
»Zollhof«, an office block built by the
American architect Frank Gehry.

»Westfälisches Versailles«: das Was- »
serschloss Nordkirchen, von einem
Fürstbischof von Münster auf einer
rechteckigen Insel erbaut.

»Westphalian Versailles«: the moated
castle of Nordkirchen was built on a
rectangular island by a prince bishop
of Münster.

Zum Wasserschloss Raesfeld mit ›
seinem 50 Meter hohen Turm gehören ein ausgedehnter Park und ein
Tiergarten aus der Renaissance.

The moated castle of Raesfeld with
its 50-metre-high tower has an extensive park and a zoological garden
from the Renaissance.

« Seit 2001 ist die Zeche Zollverein Weltkulturerbe. Das Fördergerüst über Schacht 12 ist der bekannteste Teil des ehemaligen Steinkohleberg-werks.

Since 2001 the coal-mine Zollverein has been a World Heritage site. The conveyor over shaft 12 is the most well known attraction of the former coal-mine.

« Hier wohnte Karl der Große dem Got-tesdienst bei: das weltberühmte Ok-togon der kaiserlichen Pfalzanlage in Aachen.

Here Charlemagne sat through mass: the world famous octogon in the im-perial palace in Aachen.

‹ Der Prinzipalmarkt ist die »gute Stu-be« der Stadt Münster. Aus seinen Arkadengängen blickt man auf die spätgotische Kirche St. Lamberti.

The Prinzipalmarkt is the »cosy tav-ern« of Münster. From its arcades we see the late Gothic church of St. Lamberti.

‹ Heute Weltkulturerbe: das Barock-
schloss Augustusburg in Brühl, die
prachtvolle Residenz der Kurfürsten
und Erzbischöfe von Köln.

Today a World Heritage site: the Baroque palace of Augustusburg in
Brühl, the majestic residence of the
electors and archbishops of Cologne.

‹ »Bitte ein Kölsch!« Gemütliche Bier-
gärten in der Kölner Altstadt laden
den Besucher der Rheinmetropole zu
einer Erfrischungspause ein.

»A Kölsch, please!« Pleasant beer
gardens in Cologne's old town invite
guests to refresh themselves with the
local beer.

‹ Das neue Plenargebäude in Bonn
entstand 1988 bis 1990, also noch
kurz vor der Wiedervereinigung.

The new parliament building in Bonn
was built between 1988 and 1990,
thus shortly before reunification.

« 600 Jahre Bauzeit: Der gotische Kölner Dom wurde als romantisches
Symbol der deutschen Reichseini-
gung 1880 vollendet.

600 years under construction: The
Gothic cathedral in Cologne was completed as a romantic symbol for the uni-
fication of the German Reich in 1880.

‹ Das Hochhaus unter den deutschen Burgen: Erbteilungen unter den Besitzern führten zum ständigen Ausbau der uneinnehmbaren Burg Eltz.

The »high rise« of all German castles: Division of inheritance among the owning family led to constant extensions to Eltz Castle.

« Bei Koblenz, das von der Festung Ehrenbreitstein überragt wird, mündet die Mosel am „Deutschen Eck" in den Rhein.

Near Koblenz the fortress of Ehrenbreitstein towers over the confluence of the Mosel and the Rhine at the »Deutsches Eck«.

‹ Imposantes Stadttor: Die Porta Nigra wurde um 180 in Trier erbaut.

An impressive Roman city gate: The Porta Nigra in Trier was built in 180.

« Blick auf Mayschoß, ein Zentrum des Weinbaus an der Ahr. Die Winzergenossenschaft Mayschoss-Altenahr ist die älteste Weinbaugenossenschaft der Welt.

Mayschoß, a centre of viniculture in the Ahr valley. The wine-grower's association of Mayschoß-Altenahr is the oldest wine cooperative worldwide.

Von den Weinbergen herab blickt ›
man auf die Stadt Bacharach und auf
den Verlauf des Rheins, auf dem hier
Fähren verkehren.

Looking down from the vineyards on
the town of Bacharach and the
course of the Rhine where ferries
cross.

Der älteste Renaissancebrunnen ›
Deutschlands steht auf dem Marktplatz von Mainz. Erzbischof Albrecht
von Brandenburg stiftete ihn 1526.

The oldest Renaissance fountain in
Germany stands on the market place
in Mainz. A donation by Archbishop
Albrecht of Brandenburg in 1526.

Die spätmittelalterliche Inselburg »
Pfalzgrafenstein bei Kaub kontrollier-
te einst den gesamten Warenverkehr
auf dem Rhein.

In the late Middle Ages the island
castle Pfalzgrafenstein near Kaub
once controlled all the commercial
trade on the Rhine.

≪ Rekonstruierte Fachwerkbauten säumen den Römer in Frankfurt.

Reconstructed half-timbered buildings around the Frankfurt Römer.

⌃ Mittelalterliche Skulpturen im Liebieghaus am Frankfurter Museumsufer.

Medieval sculptures in the Liebieghaus in Frankfurt's museum quarter.

Vom Frankfurter Domturm geht der ⟩ Blick über die Kunsthalle Schirn, den Römer und die Paulskirche (ganz rechts im Bild) auf die Skyline der Bankenmetropole am Main.

From the tower of Frankfurt Cathedral our view takes in the Schirn art gallery, the Römer and the Paulskirche (on the far right) against the skyline of the banking city on the Main.

⟨ Die sogenannte Königshalle in Lorsch, eines der ganz seltenen profanen Bauwerke aus karolingischer Zeit.

The so-called Königshalle in Lorsch is a rare secular building from the Carolingian period.

⌐ Die Mathildenhöhe war eine von ihren Mitgliedern selbst gestaltete Künstlerkolonie in Darmstadt und umfasst Bauwerke des deutschen Jugendstils.

The Mathildenhöhe in Darmstadt, an artists' colony, was designed by its inhabitants and presents architecture of the German Art Nouveau.

∧ Das barocke Chorgestühl im romanischen Dom von Worms, ein Werk von Balthasar Neumann, belegt die kontinuierliche Nutzung und Gestaltung des Kirchenraums.

The Baroque choir stalls in the Romanesque Worms Cathedral, a work by Balthasar Neumann, is an example for the continual use and refurbishment of the church's interior.

‹ Im Dom von Speyer, einem Haupt-
werk der deutschen Romanik, liegen
acht deutsche Kaiser und Könige be-
graben.

In Speyer Cathedral, a masterpiece
of German Romanesque architecture, eight German emperors and
kings are buried.

^ Das historische Rathaus in Deidesheim, einem Wein- und Gastronomie-
zentrum der Pfalz, wirkt wie der Inbegriff deutscher Dorfromantik.

The historic town hall in Deidesheim,
a centre of viniculture and gastrono-
my in the Palatinate, appears as the
quintessence of a romantic German
village.

DER SÜDEN |
THE SOUTH

* Baden-Württemberg, Bayern

* Baden-Wuerttemberg, Bavaria

Der Süden Deutschlands hat viel zu bieten. In Baden-Württemberg und Bayern haben viele Städte ein südländisches Flair – das Ergebnis eines regen kulturellen Austauschs mit Italien. Von Frankreich und Österreich her drangen ebenfalls künstlerische Anregungen, aber auch gastronomische Besonderheiten über Vogesen und Alpen hinweg in die südlichen Bundesländer ein. Ebenso prägend sind die fruchtbaren Landschaften der Pfalz, Schwabens und Frankens, die rauen Höhen des Schwarzwalds und die sanften Höhenzüge des Voralpenlands. Donau, Neckar und Isar gehören wie der Bodensee zu den charakteristischen Gewässern des Südens.

The south of Germany has a lot to offer. In Baden-Wuerttemberg and Bavaria many towns enjoy a southern European flair resulting from an active cultural exchange with Italy. From France and Austria, not only artistic stimuli but also gastronomic specialities came over the Vosges and the Alps to the southern regions of Germany. Impressive too are the fertile country of the Palatinate, Swabia, and Franconia, the wild and windy hill tops of the Black Forest and the softly rolling foothills of the Alps. The rivers Danube, Neckar and Isar, and Lake Constance, are among the many waterways characteristic of the south.

Hoch über dem Donautal ragt der Knopfmacherfelsen empor.

High above the valley of the Danube tower the »Knopfmacher« crags.

» Eine typische Bischofsresidenz: Über die verwinkelte Altstadt Bambergs geht der Blick zum romanischen Dom und zur einstigen Residenz.

A typical bishop's residence: The view over the quaint historic centre of Bamberg to the Romanesque cathedral and former residence.

» Die glänzendste geistliche Residenz Frankens war Würzburg. Das Schloss der Fürstbischöfe besitzt einen barocken Garten.

The most splendid ecclesiastical residence in Franconia was Würzburg. The palace of the prince-bishops has a Baroque garden.

‹ Ein Höhepunkt barocker Illusionsmalerei ist das von Giovanni Battista Tiepolo ausgemalte Treppenhaus in der Würzburger Residenz.

A highlight of Baroque illusionary art is the staircase in the Würzburg Residence painted by Giovanni Battista Tiepolo.

≋ Blick auf das Altmühltal bei Riedenburg mit Schloss Prunn in der Ferne.

View of the Altmühl Valley at Riedenburg with Prunn Castle in the distance.

⌃ Die Altstadt Nürnbergs schmiegt sich an den dominanten Burgberg.

The Old Town in Nuremberg nestles under the dominant Burgberg.

Als Inbegriff deutscher Städteroman- ›
tik gilt das wohl erhaltene Rothenburg
ob der Tauber mit seinem Fachwerk.

The epitome of a romantic German
town is the well-preserved centre of
Rothenburg ob der Tauber with its
half-timbered houses.

^ Hinter dem Brückenturm der Steinernen Brücke in Regensburg erhebt sich der gotische Dom.

The Steinerne Brücke in Regensburg leads over the Danube. Behind the bridge tower rises the Gothic cathedral.

Die Donaulandschaft bei Weltenburg ↗ bietet faszinierende Anblicke – und lädt zum Paddeln und Baden ein.

The banks of the Danube at Weltenburg offer a fascinating view – and invite one to hire a boat and go for a swim.

Die Abtei Weltenburg bei Kelheim, direkt an der Donau gelegen, gilt als ältestes Kloster Bayerns.

Weltenburg Abbey at Kelheim, lying directly beside the Danube, is said to be the oldest monastery in Bavaria.

In der Walhalla bei Regensburg sind ›
die Büsten und Statuen der großen
Deutschen aufgestellt.

In the Walhalla near Regensburg the
busts and statues of great Germans
are exhibited.

‹ Die Donaustadt Passau, Ausgangspunkt für verlockende Flusskreuzfahrten, wird von den barocken Zwiebelkuppeln des Doms überragt.

The onion domes of the cathedral tower over Passau on the Danube, departure point for enticing river cruises.

‹ Unterhalb der Veste Oberhaus – einst die Residenz der Bischöfe von Passau – fließen die Ilz und der Inn in die mächtige Donau.

Below the Veste Oberhaus – once the residence of the bishops of Passau – flow the Ilz and the Inn into the mighty Danube.

‹ Zeugnis von Frömmigkeit und Volksglauben: ein typisches Wegekreuz bei Regen im Bayerischen Wald.

Witness to piety and popular faith: a typical wayside crucifix near Regen in the Bavarian Forest.

« Romantische Flussszenerie im Bayerischen Wald bei Ottmannszell.

Romantic river scene in the Bavarian Forest near Ottmannszell.

Das Kurhaus und die Promenade in ›
Baden-Baden waren im 19. Jahrhun-
dert der Treffpunkt der mondänen
Welt.

The spa hall and the promenade in
Baden-Baden were a rendezvous for
high society in the 19th century.

An diese Stadt kann man sein Herz »
verlieren: Heidelberg mit Alter Brücke, Schloss und Heiliggeistkirche.

One can lose one's heart in this city:
Heidelberg with the Old Bridge, castle and Heiliggeistkirche.

Karlsruhe wurde ab 1715 als badische ›
Residenzstadt planmäßig angelegt.
Vom Schlossturm führen die Straßen
fächerförmig in die Umgebung.

From 1715, Karlsruhe was systemati-
cally built as the residence of Baden.
The palace tower is the centre of the
radiating streets.

Das Kloster Maulbronn gilt als frühes »
Meisterwerk der deutschen Gotik.
Hier gingen unter anderem auch Höl-
derlin und Hermann Hesse zur Schule.

The monastery of Maulbronn is an
early masterpiece of German Gothic.
Here such personalities as Hölderlin
and Hermann Hesse went to school.

☞ Blick ins Schlafzimmer von Königin Charlotte Mathilde im Schloss von Ludwigsburg, einer der weitläufigsten barocken Schlossanlagen in Deutschland.

View into the bedroom of Queen Charlotte Mathilde in Ludwigsburg, which is one of the biggest Baroque palaces in Germany.

⌐ Weinbergidyll am Stadtrand von Stuttgart. Den höchsten Punkt markiert der Rotenberg mit der Grabkapelle von Königin Katharina von Württemberg.

Romantic vineyards on the outskirts of Stuttgart, dominated by the Rotenberg with the funerary chapel for Russian-born Queen Katharina of Württemberg.

‹ Die Postmoderne ist bunt – zumindest im Fall der Stuttgarter Neuen Staatsgalerie von James Stirling.

Postmodern architecture is colourful – at least in the case of James Stirling's Neue Staatsgalerie in Stuttgart.

⌃ Bei schönem Wetter ideal für eine Pause: der große Platz zwischen Königsbau und Neuem Schloss in Stuttgarts Mitte.

Ideal for a break on sunny days: the square between King's Building and New Palace in Stuttgart's city centre.

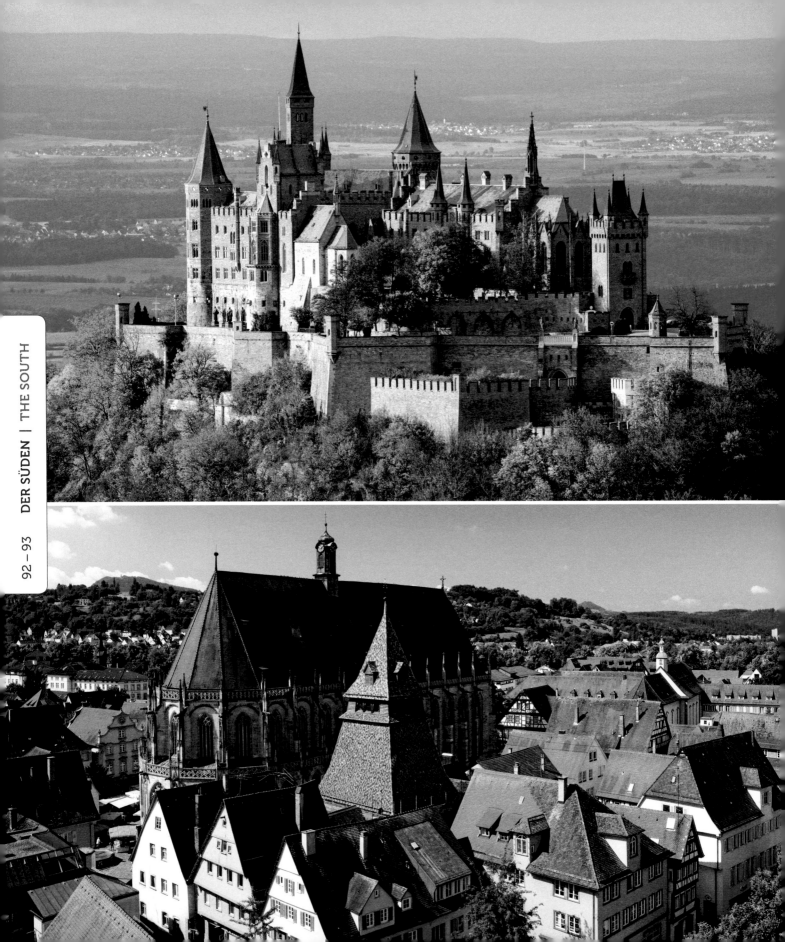

⌐ Die preußischen Hohenzollern ließen im 19. Jahrhundert ihre namengebende Stammburg bei Hechingen renovieren.

In the 19th century, the Prussian Hohenzollerns had their ancestral seat of the same name near Hechingen renovated.

‹ Schwäbisch Gmünds behagliche Altstadt wird von der spätgotischen Heiligkreuzkirche dominiert.

The pleasant Old Town of Schwäbisch Gmünd is dominated by the late-Gothic Heiligkreuzkirche (Church of the Holy Cross).

Im Sigmaringer Schloss oberhalb der ⌃ jungen Donau wohnt noch heute ein Zweig der Hohenzollern-Familie.

In Sigmaringen Castle above the young Danube, a branch of the Hohenzollern family still lives.

« Die noch genutzte Fuggerei in Augsburg wurde von dem mächtigen Kaufmannsgeschlecht der Fugger im 16. Jahrhundert als Sozialsiedlung gestiftet.

The still used »Fuggerei« in Augsburg is a donation made by the influential merchant family, the Fuggers, in the 16th century as a welfare institution for the poor and needy.

« Die Neckarfront der alten Universitätsstadt Tübingen mit dem Hölderlinturm am linken Bildrand.

The Neckar front of the old university city Tübingen with Hölderlin's Tower on the left side of the photo.

‹ Der Turm des Ulmer Münsters, das als Pfarrkirche ab 1377 errichtet wurde, ist seit seiner Vollendung 1890 der höchste Kirchturm der Welt.

The tower of Ulm Minster, built as a parish church from 1377, has been the highest spire in the world since its completion in 1890.

Die barocke Wallfahrtskirche Birnau ›
blickt über Weinberge hinab auf den
Bodensee.

The Baroque pilgrimage church
Birnau overlooks the vineyard slopes
at the Lake Constance.

Die Hafeneinfahrt der Freien Reichs- »
stadt Lindau, die 1806 an Bayern fiel,
bewacht seit 1856 ein steinerner bay-
erischer Löwe.

The harbour entrance of Lindau, a
Free Imperial City which became part
of Bavaria in 1806, is guarded by a
stone Bavarian lion.

Die Insel Reichenau im Bodensee ist ›
berühmt für ihre mittelalterlichen Kirchen: hier St. Georg in Oberzell.

The Isle of Reichenau in Lake Constance is famous for its medieval
churches: here St Georg in Oberzell.

In Unteruhldingen vermitteln die »
Pfahlbauten einen Eindruck vom Leben in der Stein- und Bronzezeit.

In Unteruhldingen the pile dwellings
disclose an impression of life in the
Stone Age and Bronze Age.

Das Siegestor in München, von König ›
Ludwig I. 1840 in Auftrag gegeben,
gehört zu dessen Ausbau der Lan-
deshauptstadt Bayerns.

The Siegestor (Victory Gate) in Munich, commissioned by King Ludwig I
in 1840, is part of his extensions of
the state capital of Bavaria.

Das Antiquarium in der Münchner ›
Residenz folgt italienischer Renaissancebaukunst und diente den bayerischen Fürsten als Museum und
Bibliothek.

The »Antiquarium« in the Munich
Residence compares closely to Ital-
ian Renaissance architecture and
served as a museum and library for
Bavarian princes.

Bayerische Gemütlichkeit: Die Bier- ›
gärten am Starnberger See sind ein
beliebtes Ausflugsziel für die Münchner.

Bavarian »Gemütlichkeit«: The beer
gardens on the shore of Lake Starn-
berg are a favourite destination for
the inhabitants of Munich.

Ein Dreiklang aus Türmen: Altes und »
Neues Rathaus und die Türme der
Frauenkirche in München.

A triad of towers: the old and new
town hall and the towers of the
Frauenkirche (Church of Our Lady),
the landmark of Munich.

‹ Blick vom Freiburger Münster auf den Marktplatz der Stadt mit dem historischen, 1532 vollendeten Kaufhaus.

View from the Freiburg Minster of the town's marketplace with the historic Kaufhaus (store) completed in 1532.

Der Ritter auf dem Röhrbrunnen in ⌃ Gengenbach zeigt das Wappen der Reichsstadt.

The knight on the Röhrbrunnen fountain in Gengenbach shows the coat of arms of the imperial town.

Ungebändigte Natur: die Lotenbach- ⌃ klamm im Schwarzwald.

Wild nature: The Lotenbachklamm (gorge) in the Black Forest.

« Ideal für eine Schwarzwaldhöhenwanderung: der Weiherkopf bei Badenweiler.

Ideal for mountain hiking in the Black Forest: The Weiherkopf near Badenweiler.

‹ Der spätgotische Schnitzalter im Breisacher Münster verblüfft durch seine filigrane, detailreiche Gestaltung.

The late-Gothic sculptured altar in Breisach Minster with its amazingly intricate and detailed wood carving.

« Eine Einladung zum Rodeln und Skilaufen: Winterlandschaft bei Schönwald.

A toboggan and skiing treat: winter landscape near Schönwald.

‹ Alemannisches Brauchtum: Beim Narrensprung in Rottweil lassen sich die historischen Masken und Kostüme der schwäbischen Fasnet studieren.

Alemannic customs: During the Narrensprung (fools' jump) in Rottweil one can study the historic masks and costumes of the Swabian Fasnet (carnival).

∧ Die schönste Dorfkirche der Welt: Die
prächtig ausgestattete Wieskirche im
bayerischen Pfaffenwinkel entstand
in der Mitte des 18. Jahrhunderts.

The most beautiful village church in
the world: the magnificently fur-
nished Wieskirche in Pfaffenwinkel in
Bavaria originated in the middle of
the 18th century.

Vorbild für Disneyland: In das Mär- ›
chenschloss Neuschwanstein zog
sich der bayerische König Ludwig II.
aus der Wirklichkeit seiner Zeit zu-
rück.

A model for Disneyland: in the fairytale castle Neuschwanstein the Bavarian King Ludwig II withdrew from
the reality of his time.

Eingebettet in eine Seenlandschaft ›
am Fuße der Alpen: das Benediktinerkloster St. Mang in Füssen.

Embedded in a lake district at the
foot of the Alps: the Benedictine
monastery of St Mang in Füssen.

Gipfelkreuz auf dem 1876 Meter ho- »
hen Iseler, dem Hausberg von Oberjoch und Bad Hindelang.

The summit cross on the top of the
1876m high Iseler, the mountain that
overlooks Oberjoch and Bad Hindelang.

In dem Schloss auf einem Hügel über ›
der Altstadt von Füssen residierten
einst die Bischöfe von Augsburg.

In the castle on a hill above the Old
Town of Füssen resided the bishops
of Augsburg.

Auf dem neugotischen Schloss Ho- »
henschwangau wuchs Ludwig II. auf,
der spätere Märchenkönig.

Ludwig II, later the fairytale king,
grew up in the Neo-Gothic castle Ho-
henschwangau.

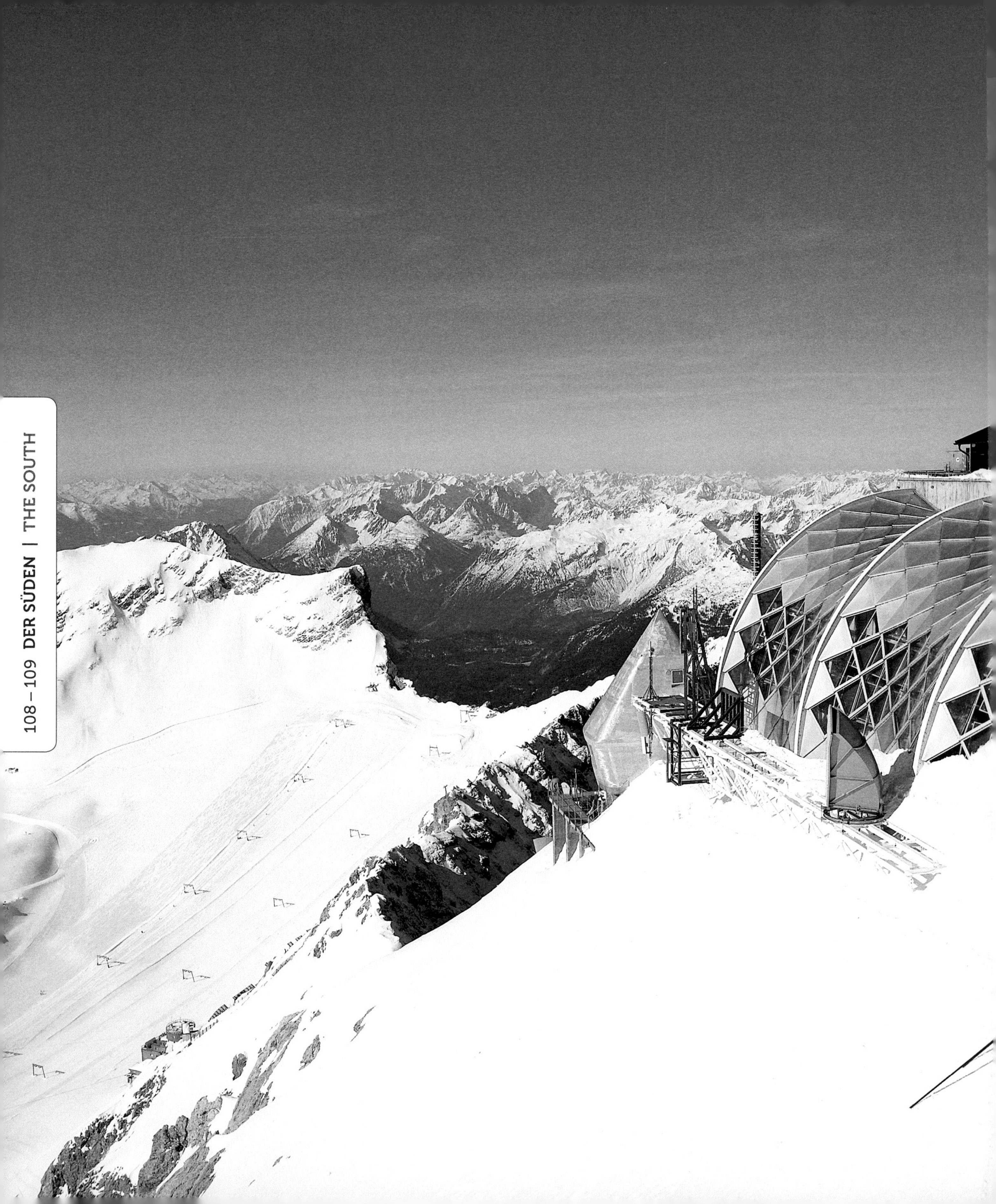

BILDNACHWEIS | PHOTO CREDITS

Titelbild	Cover	DuMont Bildarchiv/Eisele: Schloss Neuschwanstein

Buchrückseite | Back

DuMont Bildarchiv/Kreder: Kreuz auf dem Iseler bei Oberjoch, Allgäu
DuMont Bildarchiv/Lubenow: Blick auf den Kreuzaltar im Doberaner Münster
DuMont Bildarchiv/Wrba: Blick über die Elbe auf die Albrechtsburg in Meißen

Innen | Inside

Bildagentur Huber/Cozzi: 40/41 u.; Gräfenhain: 72 u., 72/73, 99; Lubenow: 66; Mirau: 38; Schmid: 77, 81, 95; Spiegelhalter: 71 u.

DuMont Bildarchiv/Bernhart: 70 u., 72 o.; Campo: 98 o.; Eisele: 98 u., 104, 108/109, 109 o., 109 u.; Fischer: 21 M., 62, 63 u., 65, 67 (3x), 90 o.; Fieselmann: 101 o., 101 u., 102 o., 102 u., 103 u.; Freyer: 39 o., 39 M., 40/41 o., 43 M., 88 o., 89 u., 103 o.; Frischmuth: 30 o., 30 u., 31 o.; Hackenberg: 3 M. u., 69 o.; Heimbach: 106 o., 106 u.; Hirth: 54 (3x), 55, 84/85, 86, 87 o., 87 u.; Holz: 74 u.; Jung: 26 o., 27 o., 27 u., 28 M., 28 u., 29; Kiedrowski: 96 o., 97 u.; Kirchner: 3 M.o., 14 o., 14 u., 15 u., 16 o., 32 o., 32 u., 33, 34 o., 34 u., 35 o., 35 u., 36/37, 57 u.; Kluyver: 98 M.; Kreder: 10, 12, 13 (3x), 21 o., 97 o, 105, 107 o., 107 u.; Knoll: 60/61; Lubenow: 3 o., 4/5, 6, 7 o., 7 M., 8 o., 8 u., 8/9, 22, 23 o., 24, 25, 26 u., 46 u., 47 u., 48, 51 o., 52, 53 o., 53 u.; Lueger: 64 o., 85 o.; Maeritz: 80 o., 82 u.; Marczok: 7 u., 16 M.; Scheibner: 21 u., 58 o., 80 u.; Schmid: 3 u., 78/79, 90 M., 90 u., 90/91, 92 u., 92 o., 93; Schröder: 19 u.; Schulz: 15 o., 47 o, 49, 51 u.; Selbach: 68 o., 69 u.; Siemers: 17, 18, 19 o.; Synnatschke Photography: 44 o., 44 u., 45 o., 45 u.; Widmann: 82 o., 85 M., 87 M.; Wrba: 56, 57 o., 57 M., 59 o., 59 u.

Fotolia/irish: 74 u.; Otta: 20; RRA: 94 o.; vvoe: 64 u.

iStockphoto.com/Benedek: 83; Frank: 88 u.; Gryankina: 63 o.; irekkrak: 28 o.; interlight: 16 u.; sborisov: 89 o.; TommL: 43 o.

laif/Knechte: 42; Steinhilber: 50

Look/Schoenen: 100/101

Mauritius/Bärnsch: 74/75; Fischer: 58 u.; Hänel: 70/71 o.; Higuchi: 46 o.; Lehner: 11 u.; Lubenow: 68 u.; FB Rose: 94 u.; Weber: 76

Pixelio/Bergmüller: 31 u.; Eder: 85 u.; Ermel: 11 o.; Großmann: 96 u.; Struck: 23 u.; Trampert: 39 u.

Stiftung Preußische Schlösser und Gärten Berlin-Brandenburg/Ibbeken: 43 u.

IMPRESSUM | IMPRINT

Covergestaltung | Cover Layout
Ingo Juergens, Südgrafik, Stuttgart

Bildredaktion, Satz | Editor
Hans-Joachim Schneider, Köln

Text | Text
Frank Druffner, Stuttgart

Übersetzung | Translation
Robert Peart, Esslingen

Karte | Map
DuMont Reisekartografie,
Fürstenfeldbruck

Repro | Repro
Pre Print Partner GmbH & Co. KG, Köln

Druck | Print
Printed in Germany

MIX
Papier aus verantwor-
tungsvollen Quellen
FSC® C012425
FSC
www.fsc.org

2. Auflage 2014 | 2nd edition 2014
ISBN 978-3-7701-8938-0

© DuMont Reiseverlag GmbH & Co. KG,
Marco-Polo-Str. 1, 73760 Ostfildern
www.dumontreise.de

INDEX

REGISTER

‹ Die Zugspitze ist mit 2962 Metern der höchste Berg Deutschlands – das Münchner Haus bietet Unterkunft.

At 2962 meters, the Zugspitze is the highest mountain in Germany – the Münchner Haus offers accommodation.

Das Benediktinerkloster Ettal ist ein ≫ beeindruckender Zentralbau.

The Benedictine monastery of Ettal is an impressive building with a central ground-plan.

Blumen und Fresken: typische Häuser ˄ in Garmisch-Partenkirchen.

Flowers and frescoes: typical houses in Garmisch-Partenkirchen.